Made in the USA
Las Vegas, NV
09 October 2021

31976347R00066